I0820805

Octopuses

by Chris Bowman

BLASTOFF! READERS, AN IMPRINT OF BELLWETHER MEDIA BY FLUTTERBEE

Blastoff! Readers are carefully developed by literacy experts to build reading stamina and move students toward fluency by combining standards-based content with developmentally appropriate text.

Level 1 provides the most support through repetition of high-frequency words, light text, predictable sentence patterns, and strong visual support.

Level 2 offers early readers a bit more challenge through varied sentences, increased text load, and text-supportive special features.

Level 3 advances early-fluent readers toward fluency through increased text load, less reliance on photos, advancing concepts, longer sentences, and more complex special features.

Reading Level

Grade K

Grades 1–3

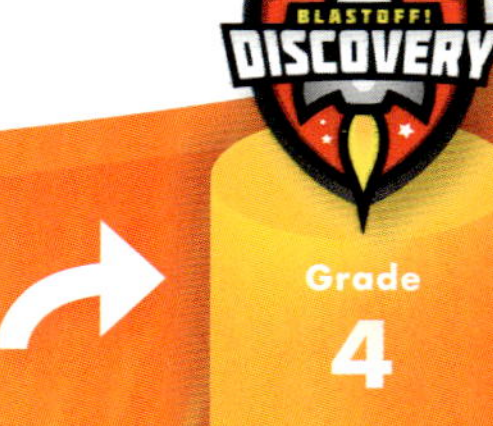

Grade 4

This edition first published in 2026 by Bellwether Media, Inc.

Library of Congress Cataloging-in-Publication Data is available at www.loc.gov or upon request from the publisher.

ISBN: 9798893047967 (hardcover)
ISBN: 9798893048964 (ebook)

Editor: Kieran Downs Designer: Brittany McIntosh

Printed in the United States of America, North Mankato, MN.

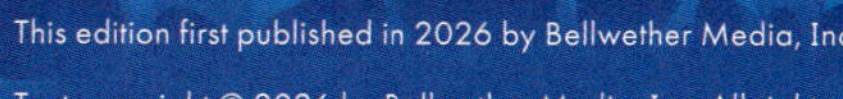

Table of Contents

What Are Octopuses? 4
Sneaky Swimmers 12
Growing Up 18
Glossary 22
To Learn More 23
Index 24

What Are Octopuses?

Octopuses are ocean animals. They are found in deep and **shallow** waters around the world. They are known for their eight arms.

Common Octopus Report

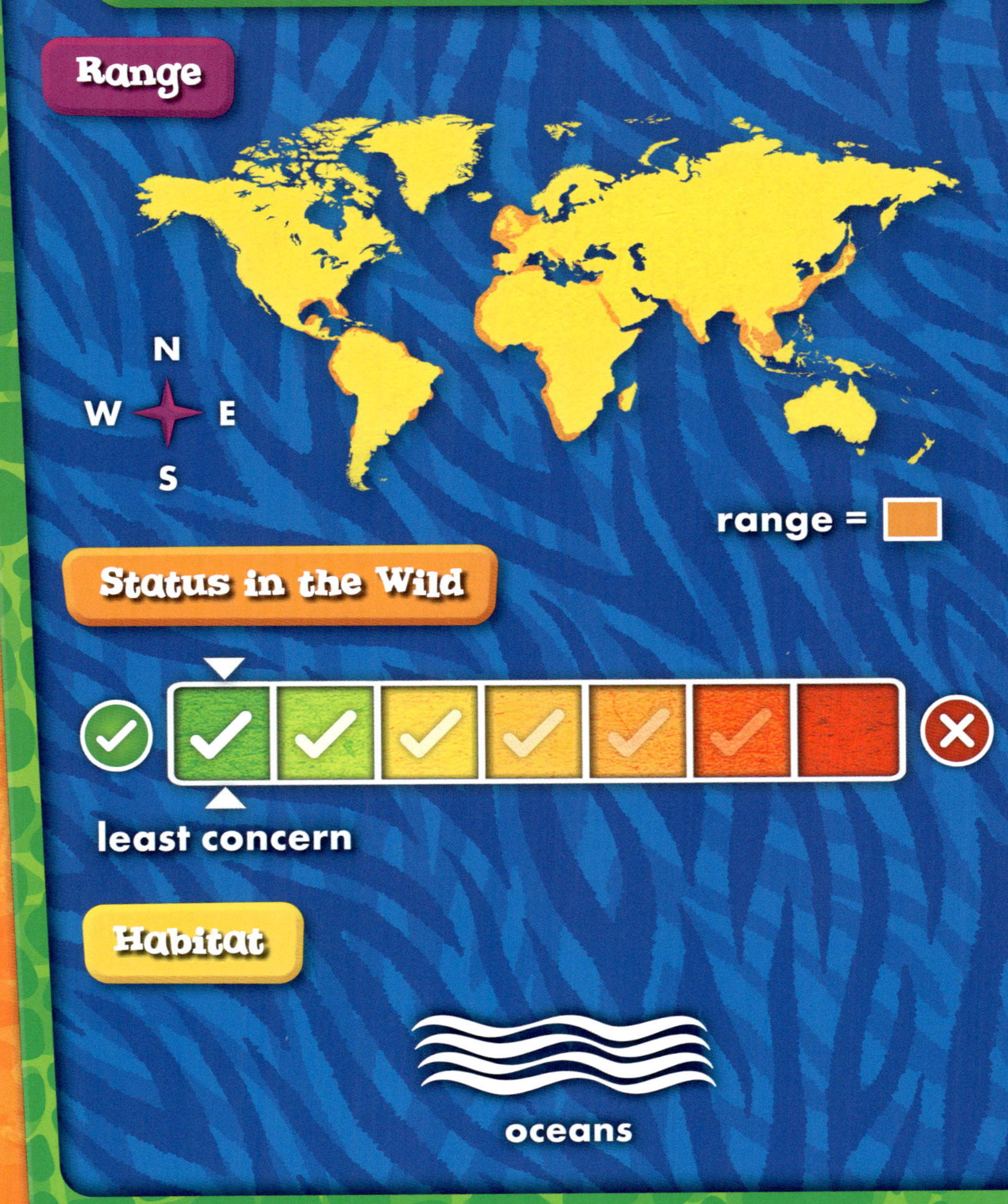

Octopuses have **suction cups** on their arms. Most use their arms to walk on the seafloor.

siphon

They also move by shooting water through their **siphons**.

Octopuses have rounded bodies and large eyes.

Their mouths are on the underside of their bodies. Their hard **beaks** help them break shells.

Some octopuses are very small. Others can be very large.

They have no bones. This helps them fit into tight spaces.

Spot an Octopus
rounded body
large eyes
arms

Sneaky Swimmers

Octopuses often live near **coasts**. Many octopuses live in **coral reefs**.

They usually live alone. They stay in **dens** to hide from **predators**.

Octopuses shoot out ink.
This lets them escape predators.

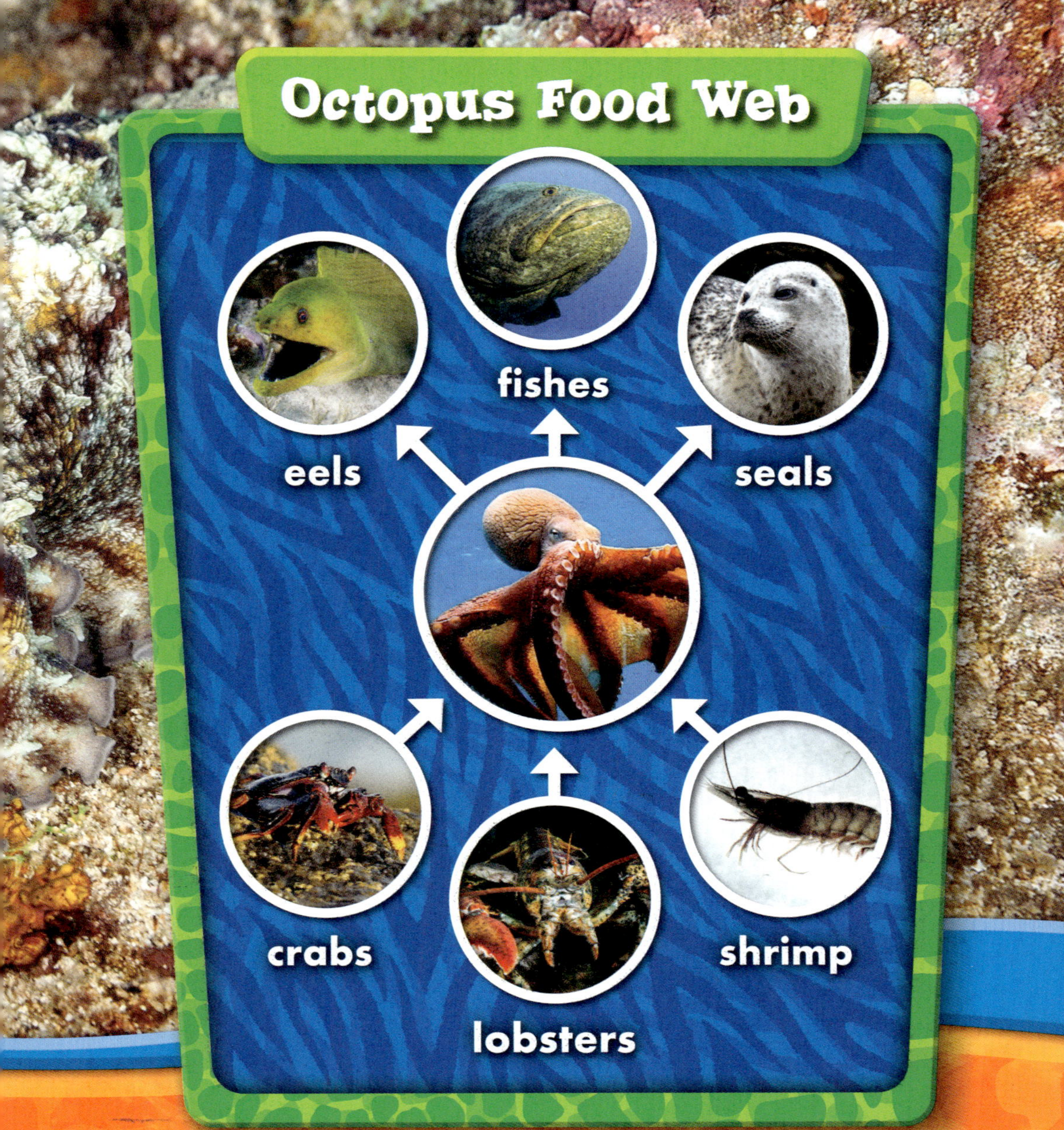

Octopuses can change their skin color. This helps them hide from eels, fishes, and seals.

Octopuses often catch meals along the ocean floor.

They search for crabs and lobsters.
Shrimp make a quick snack.

Growing Up

Female octopuses lay eggs in dens. They can lay hundreds of thousands of eggs at a time.

Females guard the eggs until they **hatch**. Small **larvae** come out.

larva

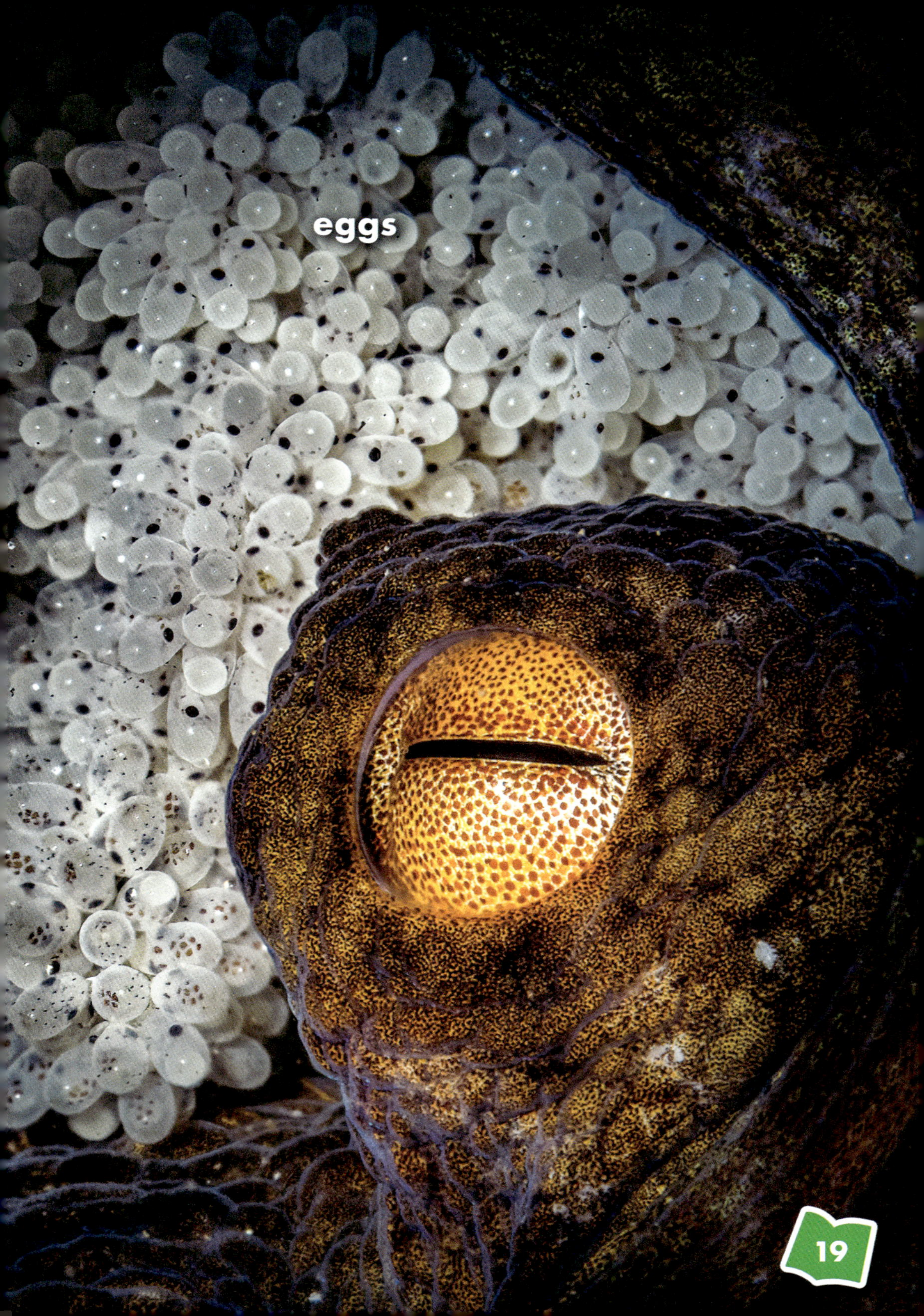
eggs

Octopus larvae can swim and eat right away.

Most move towards the ocean floor as they grow. Time to find a den!

Life of an Octopus

Name of Babies

larvae

Number of Eggs

up to 500,000

Time Spent in Eggs

4 to 8 weeks or more

Life Span

Glossary

beaks—the mouths of some animals

coasts—areas of water near the shore

coral reefs—groups of corals that grow in warm, shallow ocean waters

dens—sheltered places

hatch—to break open

larvae—baby octopuses that have just hatched from eggs

predators—animals that hunt other animals for food

shallow—not deep

siphons—tubes that octopuses use to move in the water

suction cups—flexible circles that can stick to many surfaces

To Learn More

AT THE LIBRARY

Mattern, Joanne. *Octopuses.* Minneapolis, Minn.: Bellwether Media, 2021.

Murray, Julie. *Octopuses.* Minneapolis, Minn.: ABDO, 2022.

Sabelko, Rebecca. *Ocean Animals.* Minneapolis, Minn.: Bellwether Media, 2023.

ON THE WEB

FACTSURFER

Factsurfer.com gives you a safe, fun way to find more information.

1. Go to www.factsurfer.com.
2. Enter "octopuses" into the search box and click 🔍.
3. Select your book cover to see a list of related content.

Index

arms, 4, 6, 11
beaks, 9
bodies, 8, 9, 11
coasts, 12
coral reefs, 12
dens, 13, 18, 21
eggs, 18, 19, 21
eyes, 8, 11
larvae, 18, 20, 21
predators, 13, 14
siphons, 7
suction cups, 6

The images in this book are reproduced through the courtesy of: Rich Carey, front cover, p. 11; ver0nicka, pp. 2-3; Andrea Izzotti, p. 3; Martin Strmiska/ Alamy Stock Photo, p. 4; David Lee, p. 6 (top); Mike Veitch/ Alamy Stock Photo, p. 6; Jonathan Hernould, p. 7; Bruyu, p. 8; Dorling Kindersley ltd/ Alamy Stock Photo, p. 9 (top); Aerial-motion, p. 9; Gerald Robert Fischer, p. 10; John A. Anderson, pp. 10-11; Richard Whitcombe, p. 12; Sahara Frost, p. 13; deraugenzeuge, pp. 14-15; Karel Bartik, p. 15 (eels); Jesus Cobaleda, p. 15 (fishes); grafxart, p. 15 (seals); Amirkhans world, p. 15 (octopus); Martin Pelanek, p. 15 (crabs); RLS Photo, p. 15 (lobsters); Unknown/ Wikipedia, p. 15 (shrimp); ANESTIS REKKAS/ Alamy Stock Photo, p. 16; DiveIvanov, p. 17; Andre-Johnson, p. 18; kkshxt, pp. 18-19; Bass Supakit, p. 20; SergeUWPhoto, p. 21; JonMilnes, p. 23.